EXPRESS YOURSELF WITH
COLOR

Better Homes and Gardens® Books
Des Moines, Iowa

Better Homes and Gardens® Books
An imprint of Meredith® Books

Express Yourself with Color
Project Editor: Linda Hallam
Contributing Editor: Heather Lobdell
Art Director: Jerry J. Rank
Copy Editor: Carol Boker
Proofreaders: Christina Hoenig, Deborah Morris Smith
Editorial and Design Assistants: Jennifer Norris, Karen Schirm, Barbara A. Suk
Production Director: Douglas M. Johnston
Production Manager: Pam Kvitne
Assistant Prepress Manager: Marjorie J. Schenkelberg

Meredith® Books
Editor in Chief: James D. Blume
Design Director: Matt Strelecki
Managing Editor: Gregory H. Kayko
Executive Shelter Editor: Denise L. Caringer

Director, Sales & Marketing, Retail: Michael A. Peterson
Director, Sales & Marketing, Special Markets: Rita McMullen
Director, Sales & Marketing, Home & Garden Center Channel: Ray Wolf
Director, Operations: Valerie Wiese

Vice President, General Manager: Jamie L. Martin

Better Homes and Gardens® Magazine
Editor in Chief: Jean LemMon
Executive Interior Design Editor: Sandra S. Soria

Meredith Publishing Group
President, Publishing Group: Christopher M. Little
Vice President, Consumer Marketing & Development: Hal Oringer

Meredith Corporation
Chairman and Chief Executive Officer: William T. Kerr
Chairman of the Executive Committee: E. T. Meredith III

Cover photograph: Gordon Beall. The room is shown on *pages 50-51*.

All of us at Better Homes and Gardens® Books are dedicated to providing you with information and ideas you need to enhance your home. We welcome your comments and suggestions about this book on color. Write to us at: Better Homes and Gardens® Books, Shelter Department, RW–206, 1716 Locust St., Des Moines, IA 50309–3023.

EXPRESS YOURSELF WITH COLOR CONTENTS

COLOR IS ONE OF THE CONSTANTS in our lives. We learn, work, think, and dream in color. From the time we wake until we go to sleep, we live among the ever-changing colors of nature—from the pale roses of sunrise to the vibrant oranges and purples of sunset to the inky black of night. From earliest childhood, we all have natural color preferences, favorite colors that warm our lives and soothe our souls.

GETTING STARTED

COLOR OPTIONS
*Color, color everywhere and just the right shades for your home and personal style.
If you don't find the color or color palette you want in one of the featured photographs, the alternative four-color block chips throughout each chapter expand your choices.
The blocks help you see more colors—and illustrate lively combinations.*

These colors lift our moods or remind us of pleasant memories. A sunny yellow recalls family times in the kitchen; a cool green, our grandmother's favorite vase. That's the joy of color. We can create our own environments based on the colors that make us happy.

In Chapter One, we start at the beginning—how to create a color palette from your real-life possessions. If you aren't sure what works for you, take the Discovering Your Inner Hue quiz, page 21. Or, if you aren't certain how the orientation, location, siting, and features of your home affect choices, see the Whose Hue to Use? checklist on page 40. Whatever your color passions turn out to be, you'll find examples throughout the seven chapters. Remember, the best thing about color is this: Colors that inspire and comfort don't cost any more than dull ones. Surround yourself and fill your home with the colors you love.

CLOCKWISE FROM TOP LEFT:

If you've lived with neutral colors for a long time or are just starting the adventure of decorating your home, work into color at your own comfortable pace. As you study the photographs throughout this book, you'll find easy ways to introduce color. If deep blues or reds seem like too much, turn to the warming power of yellow. This always-happy color is a natural for everything from dining to sleeping. For a quick initiation into color, start with a few accents, such as the pottery vases. Begin with a small, easy-to-paint room, such as this decoratively painted bath. Or, introduce a plaid chair and cushion (or just accent pillows) into a neutral living room. Paint guest room window frames in a bold color. And warm a bath with just a hint of delicate color.

ABOVE: *When your living and dining rooms flow into each other, think blending, but not necessarily identical color schemes. Here, the living room walls are a lighter shade of the taupe used in the adjoining dining room, handsomely framed by the cased opening. For visual harmony, trim color (or stain) and flooring should match when rooms open to each other.*

RIGHT: *For an exact color match, roll up your rug and take it along to a paint store. Consider that colors look different on walls than on floors. To be safe, have a test pint mixed and paint a square before doing your room. You might want to go lighter or darker.*

TRIED & TRUE

Even if you are moving into a new house, it's unlikely you'll start totally from scratch when you choose your color palette and paint colors. Usually, you are working with some givens—a favorite painting, upholstered furniture, collections of pottery or plates—or, in the recently redecorated older home shown here, a handsome needlepoint rug. Pulling a wall color from a rug is a favorite tried-and-true decorator trick, as wall colors are easy to mix. And, shopping for a rug to match or blend with an existing wall color is notoriously difficult. Here, the homeowner took full advantage of the shades of taupe and black in a living room rug purchased for a previous house. For the color palette, three wall shades emerged that work well with existing furniture and art. The lighter taupe creates a serene background for collected furnishings and regional art in the living room. A darker shade of taupe, paired with slate black, gives instant drama to a previously small, drab dining room. The stylish two-tone effect emulates the look of wainscoting at the cost of a can of paint.

ABOVE: *Take advantage of an existing chair rail and enliven your dining room with two complementary colors. Contrast lighter and darker colors for drama. If you like a subtle look, choose two shades of the same color. To visually anchor the space, paint the darker color or shade below the chair rail to give the effect of painted wainscoting.*

ABOVE: *Consider accessories and fabrics when you are searching for a mood-creating wall color. Here, the rusty red in a collection of pillows, sewn from kilim rug fragments, inspired the wall color for a guest room. The red gives a mellow background for the roughly textured kilim patterns. To avoid overwhelming a bedroom with such saturated color, pair it with white blinds and woodwork and a pale duvet, shown here.*

TOP RIGHT: *Only an accent in this oversize pillow, cobalt blue energizes dated paneling in a small family room. (For more on painting paneling, see page 111.)*

RIGHT: *Trying to unify a number of elements into one decorating scheme? Employ the unifying power of color. Here a deep, burgundy-hued red repeats accents in the floral pillows as well as the richer tones of the small oil painting. The color also helps to frame the small painting, which is hung at eye level for enjoyment.*

COLOROPTIONS ■ *Like dark, dramatic colors but want more choices? Instead of cobalt blue, look at a rich, clear shade of green for saturated, dramatic color. Or if the reds here don't work for you, explore purple, deep lavender, and brick shades for room-creating backdrops that instantly give style and mood to your setting.*

COLOR**OPTIONS**

New homes and townhouses are often light and white inside–a blank canvas for creativity. Here, a color-craving homeowner started with definite givens—multicolored, floral-patterned upholstered furniture and a vaulted living room with adjoining, open dining area. For no-fail living room wall color, she matched a honey-gold shade in the sofa fabric to stock wall color on a paint chip chart. When you pull a color from fabric, consider how it will appear as a wall color. In a bedroom or smaller room, the shades of rose or teal from this fabric would be appealing. To give the dining room interest, especially at night, the owner chose a paint color two shades darker on the chip. This trick guarantees compatible shades. For a touch of shine, paint is a satin, rather than a flat finish.

ONE–STEP WONDER

BEFORE

COLOROPTIONS

LEFT: *Consider how and when you use a room before you select your palette and specific colors. If you use a dining room primarily at night with chandelier light or candlelight, think about a darker or more intense shade of your color choice. Look at test swatches at night with artificial light to make sure you are happy with your choices.*

ABOVE: *Before repainting, the open rooms appeared stark and uninviting and cold during the winter months.*

RIGHT: *Think beyond fabric to stained or natural woods when you are choosing paint color. Here the pale honey shade gives a warm, soft backdrop both to the oak mantel and the traditional Windsor-style chair.*

COLOROPTIONS ■ *If a honey gold doesn't work with your scheme, other easy-to-live-with choices include shades of terra-cotta, warm stone grays, or clear medium greens or blues. Choose midrange colors for pleasing, not attention-grabbing backdrops.*

ROOM REVIVAL

Nothing rescues older homes–and families on tight budgets–faster than fresh paint. Here, an existing rug sets the agenda for a vibrant color scheme. In a previous home, the cranberry-and-navy kilim rug anchored a pale terra-cotta room. In a much smaller living room with white-painted grasscloth walls, small windows, and a stone fireplace, the rug dominated (see before). To balance the strong cranberry red, the owners decided to try an equally intense wall color. They taped up paint chips in numerous shades of red, eventually narrowing their choices to three shades. Before making the final commitment, they painted swatches of paint above the sofa and mantel (see left). One red was obviously too rusty, the other too bright. Fortunately, as with the little bear's porridge, one stock shade was just right. For extra depth of color, as the room is often used for entertaining at night, they chose a semigloss finish. If you prefer not to call attention to wall texture, such as this painted grasscloth, or to less-than-perfect walls, use flat paint.

LEFT: *Not ready for a wall test? Paint your choices on poster board and lean or tape in place to study the effects of light on your colors.*

OPPOSITE TOP LEFT: *Take advantage of moving as an opportunity to rethink your color choices. Here, a rug that worked fine in another house overpowered this small room. Because of the long, harsh winters, the owners turned to red paint to warm the cool room.*

ABOVE: *With the rug balanced by the wall color, the stone fireplace takes its rightful place as the focal point. In soft lamp light, the room glows at night. Such intense color can look harsh with bright ceiling-mounted lighting. If you like overhead light, install a dimmer for control.*

COLOR**OPTIONS**

BEFORE

ABOVE: *With no kindred hues, the golden table and chairs looked lost against the gray-toned paper.*
LEFT: *Why yellow? Existing blue-and-white toile drapery panels needed a home in this cottage. Yellow unifies the blue of the fabric and the wood of the table and chairs.*
RIGHT: *Which shades? As the family had a Country French-style iron chandelier, they looked at paint chips with the warm, earthy undertones of mustard often used with this look. After removing the floral wallpaper (see page 110 for how-tos), they painted the wall above the chair rail in a pale mustard. Rather than remove the painted grasscloth, they painted it in a darker shade of the same yellow. Chair rail and ceiling molding are white, matching the crown molding.*
COLOROPTIONS ■ *For a cool but dramatic look, try the popular duo of blue and green or the charm of blue or green with gray.*

PRIMARY SECONDARY

TERTIARY MONOCHROMATIC

Why use the color wheel? This classic method helps you create a no-fail color palette. When you are beginning to decorate with color or when you are changing your palette, start with your favorite color and work with schemes based on the groupings of primary, secondary, tertiary, and monochromatic. Choose only one color as your focus and allow colors in your chosen group to be accents. (See the color wheel here.) When you stay within one classic grouping, you aren't clashing colors even in the brightest primaries. Or, even easier, choose a favorite and add close and easy-to-relate color wheel neighbors as congenial accents. Use white for relief and black for sophisticated accents.

THE COLOR WHEEL

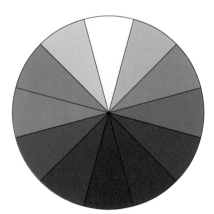

PRIMARY: Color your decorating with the classic crayon primaries of red, yellow, and blue. When used in the same intensities and in varying amounts, the three are a natural for cheerful, family-friendly rooms. For the power of a single primary color, choose your favorite of the three and balance it with wood tones and neutral accents.

SECONDARY: Green is from blue and yellow, orange from yellow and red, and purple from red and blue. You'll likely look beyond the clearest secondary colors to tints and shades. Green is enjoying a revival. The look can be light or lively depending on the shades and accents you choose. Often tricky, sponged shades of orangy terra-cotta brighten dark green walls.

TERTIARY: Depending on your perspective, color gets fun or a little tricky at this third stage. Now we are into the equal mixes of primary plus its closest secondary color—blue-green, yellow-green, red-orange, red-purple, and blue-purple. Or, try the look without major color commitment by adding tertiary touches, such as the blue-purple pillows, to a neutral scheme.

MONOCHROMATIC: Remember one-color decorating isn't one-shade or one-tint decorating. It also isn't restricted to neutrals. Instead you are using one color that appeals to you and introducing variations in texture and materials and in shades and tints.

DISCOVERING YOUR INNER HUE

The colors of your everyday life have a profound effect on your moods and emotions even when you're not aware of them. You associate just about everything you do, the places you occupy, what you wear, and what you own with particular colors. And each of these brings with it feelings, moods, and memories—excited or calm, energizing or restful, pleasant or unpleasant.

Do you want to open your eyes to your true color feelings—and put the emotional power of color association to work for you? Complete the following fun and informative inventory of activities and related colors. Use a separate sheet of paper and compare the results with a friend. Then calculate your color preferences and use the results to help you decorate your home into the happiest environment possible. When you know your own personal color associations, you can surround yourself with the shades that reflect your moods throughout the day and that enhance the purpose of every room in your home.

COLOR AND ACTIVITY INVENTORY

For insight on your color preferences, think about the color you associate with the listed activities: *Ask yourself what color you would like to wear or be surrounded by as you do it.*

Color Choice

1. Going to bed — *blue* B
2. Eating breakfast — *Yellow Sunshine* A
3. Lounging in your bathrobe — *Pale Blue* B
4. Soaking in the tub — *" "* B
5. Applying make-up — *White* C
6. Polishing your nails — *"* C
7. Driving in your car — *Soft Gray* C
8. Picking field flowers — *Red - Bluebonnets* B
9. Harvesting your garden — *Green* B
10. Coloring your hair — *Brown* C
11. Tying a scarf or tie — *"* C
12. Setting the table — *Wood brown* C
13. Going to a fancy ball — *Black/white* C
14. Eating at your favorite restaurant — *Tan/brown* C
15. Lighting a candelabra for a romantic dinner — *Tan/brown,* C
16. Putting up the patio umbrella — *Blue/white* A
17. Placing a wreath on the front door — *Green* B
18. Sitting with a refreshing drink — *Blue* B
19. Reading in front of the fire — *Brown* C
20. Mowing the lawn — *Green* B
21. Dressing for work — *Blue/brown* C
22. Biking with friends — *Black* C
23. Swimming in the ocean — *Dusk Tan/Pink* C
24. Jogging after work — *Black* C
25. Kayaking down a river — *"* C
26. Daydreaming at home — *Tan/brown* C
27. Cooking for the holidays — *Beige* B
28. Talking on the telephone with your best friend — *blue* B
29. Dining with good friends — *Blue/white* B
30. Celebrating getting the job — *Red Plaid* A
31. Holding a wine tasting — *" "* A
32. Attending a country wedding — *" "* A
33. Arranging a bowl of fruit — *Blue* B
34. Critiquing a favorite painting — *Brown* C

Sept 20[01] 2000

SCORING

Now designate each of your color choices according to three basic categories of color association—*warm, cool, and neutral colors*. First, find your colors in the following category lists:

Warm Colors: Red, Orange, Yellow, Pink

Cool Colors: Blue, Green, Purple

Neutral Colors: Black, Brown, White, Gray, Beige, Taupe

Next, assign an "A" wherever you have listed a *warm* color, a "B" for all your *cool* color choices, and a "C" for *neutral* colors. Count how many you listed in each category.

Use the information below to see what your choices may say about you and where you can use colors to your advantage in every room of your home.

Your Tally: Warm __5__ Cool __12__ Neutral __17__

SCORING KEY FOR COLOR CATEGORIES

Warm Colors: Active colors that move forward, communicate vigor, cheer you up, excite passions, inspire conversation, and force emotions.

Cool Colors: Passive colors that recede into the background, cool you down, calm your nerves, lift your spirits, promote meditation, and generally comfort the soul.

Neutral Colors: Open-minded colors that are easy on the eye, symbolize a down-to-earth attitude, make you feel safe and secure, and lend a cooperative air.

HOW DO YOU COMPARE?

• *Mostly "A"s?* You come alive with energizing colors. Use these in the active rooms of your home: entryways, hallways, dining rooms, rooms for entertaining, and playrooms. Also, enliven neutral rooms with a warm accent color.

• *Mostly "B"s?* You respond to soothing colors. Use them in rooms for rest and relaxation such as the bedroom, living room, home office, spa, or sun porch.

• *Mostly "C"s?* You like to play it safe. Neutral colors are perfect for rooms that connect to other rooms, or rooms where you spend a great deal of time, such as kitchens and bathrooms.

• *Tie with two or all categories?* Evenly distribute your color "temperatures" throughout your home in doses that are compatible to the room's purpose. Bridge warm and cool colors with neutrals.

IF YOU AREN'T SURE HOW MUCH COLOR you want in your life, think about how you use color. If you collect pottery or porcelains or if you just enjoy a particular color, you have the tools to introduce and blend inspiring touches of colors throughout your home. Here and on the next four pages, the subtle greens and yellows of Depression-era pottery inspired the living and dining room color schemes. Walls and trim remain safely white. Choose two complementary colors for interesting, versatile accents when the backdrop remains white or a subtle neutral.

CREATE
COMFORT

Start at your own comfort level. Here, the muted yellow tones soften the scheme with the window treatment and gathered chandelier cord. Accessories, such as the mirror and candleholders, contrast with texture and form.

Part of the fun of decorating is in experimenting. When you start with a neutral backdrop and noncolors of wood and iron, even tiny touches stand out. If you are beginning a room or updating colors, begin with small easy-to-change touches. Here, the yellow and green accents could be phase one of enriching a room with color. When you are comfortable with your first forays, add more accents from your chosen color or branch out into other hues that blend or contrast. See color options (page 26) for more choices.

COLOR WITHOUT COMMITMENT

LEFT: *When color comes from a collection of objects, such as the pottery in this corner cupboard, group the pieces for impact. The effect is strong and attention-getting and avoids the haphazard look of small objects placed around a room. Repeat your accent colors, too, for unity. Here, the glasses on the table and the simple window treatment unify the scheme without disturbing the harmony. Accent pillows and throws are quick-to-add and easy-to-change elements that reinforce color choices.*

ABOVE: *When you play two accent colors— here yellow and green—against a neutral scheme, choose one as your primary player. To warm the room above, yellow does double duty as the window treatment and the glassware. Touches of red would further enliven and warm the scheme for cozy fireside entertaining. Or simply switching to a green window treatment and glasses would create a cooler, more summery look. With subtle backdrops, small color changes count.*

ABOVE: *Consider how adjoining rooms relate to each other. For interesting variation in the living room, the greens and golden yellows are bleached (lightened) a bit from the dining room (page 25). Melon is added to energize the mix. For the most versatility, keep your sofa neutral and introduce color with an armchair and accent pillows. The armchair fabric repeats as accent pillows. Repeat colors at least twice to tie the scheme together.*

RIGHT: *As you introduce touches of color, experiment with adding textures and subtle patterns, too. For a quick accent, drape a soft throw over a sofa or chair. Or, introduce such details as the decoupaged lampshade, stacked, framed prints, and fresh flowers.*

OPPOSITE: *Use creative touches, such as the drapery panels, to maximize small focuses of color. Interest comes from the scale and shapes.*

COLOROPTIONS ▣ *Want more accent choices for neturals? If you like colors that warm, consider these shades from orange to yellow-green.*

Even if you prefer white walls, you can live with more color than you think. For a quick start, group your most colorful accessories, such as pottery, quilts, art, and pillows. Just the addition of a flea market piece or two may be enough to fill out your more colorful scheme. If you like the idea of vibrant wall color, test the waters by painting one accent wall in your color choice. Later, if the shade feels right to you, you can finish the job or even paint the other walls in another complementary color.

NEUTRAL BEGINNINGS

OPPOSITE: *Repeat colors for a feeling of pleasing unity. Rather than a hodge-podge collection of disparate objects, this room feels carefully planned. The repeated shades of blue and green from the paintings set the tone for the pottery and charmingly distressed, odd-size shutters.*

LEFT: *Paint a wall or part of a wall in a bold (or more discreet) color and see how you live with the color. For a pulled-together look, repeat your focal-point color in smaller doses, such as always-effective pillows and candles.*

BELOW: *One jolt of color wakes up a neutral room. Here, flowers in the still life painting and red in the quilts inspired the oversized pillow.*

COLOR OPTIONS ■ *Small touches of an interesting color wake up a room. Consider purples, teals, and deep pinks as alternatives to red or blue.*

COLOR**OPTIONS**

WORKING WITH WHITE

COLOR OPTIONS

When your goal is light and airy, start with white. White walls and trim work—anywhere in your home. Because your walls aren't competing, you're free to introduce colors through your choices of fabrics, art, and accessories. Keep in mind the many, many variations of white, from the cool and stark to the warm and soft. Just as you would with color, experiment with several shades of white to find the right one for your room. If you are using white in a sun-filled room, remember to look at your color samples at different times of the day and at night with artificial light. In all-white rooms, such as these sun porches, vary the whites from cool to warm for interest. As white can appear cold, use textures and accents, such as homey quilts, pottery, baskets, and plants for inviting warmth.

LEFT: *Make the most of the freedom of white walls and furnishings to introduce a mix of pretty florals and patchwork fabrics. For a relaxed look, rather than a jarring contrast, choose patterned fabrics that include whites and pastels. If you prefer a tailored, crisper look, you can't go wrong with a sporty red, white, and blue scheme. (See page 84 for ideas.)*

ABOVE: *When your idea of a library leans to porch decor rather than dark paneling, paint the built-ins white and add white furniture, such as these always-classic wicker pieces. Use fabrics, such as the quilt, for a cozy, curl-up-and-read ambience.*

RIGHT: *Plant-filled sunrooms and sun porches are traditionally white and with good reason. Color would be a distraction where windows frame views and blur the distinction between indoors and out.*

COLOROPTIONS *It's always summer when you pair pretty pastels with white. Add touches of gray to give a white and pastel room a more sophisticated edge.*

When you're ready to introduce color into your home and favor a country look, think fabrics and patterns. New and vintage quilts and the colors of country-style fabrics are perfect ways to quickly bring spark and snap to a neutral background. To create your own look, start with your favorite collected quilt or two and pull out the most appealing colors. You'll find you naturally gravitate to bright primary colors or to soft pastels, which will set your scheme. To get the most color impact from your decorating, use a quilt as a wall hanging or as an instant cover-up for a sofa or chair. Or, skirt a round table with a quilt or with a complementary cotton print or floral.

TOUCHES
OF COUNTRY

COLOROPTIONS

OPPOSITE: *Decorated with a collection of quilts and an array of pillows, a subtle, neutral scheme now brims with bright color. Red, the ultimate warm color, pulls the mix of styles and patterns together. Caution: When you hang a quilt, protect the colors you love from sun fading by making sure it isn't in direct sunlight.*

ABOVE: *Want color without fuss in a bedroom or guest room? Hang a quilt as the focal-point headboard and dress the beds in decorative pillows of all sizes, textures, and patterns. Recycle the scraps of old quilt fragments into extra accent pillows.*

COLOROPTIONS ■ *When a country scheme is in netural, warm it with the colors of autumn leaves and falls woods. Shades of pumpkin and forest and leaf greens mix easily with rich bark brown.*

HINTS OF GOLD

Enrich ever-versatile, ever-stylish white with the power of metallic gold. As gold is such a powerful attention-getter, just a few touches are sufficient to play against white walls, a light floor, and pristine white upholstery. For easy touches, consider an oversized framed mirror and a gilded chair or table. Or, as gold accessories are readily available, add such touches as a throw, small silk accent pillows, candlesticks, porcelains, pottery pieces, a lamp base, or picture frames. The trick is restraint: Use no other colors in the room— white for the walls and major furniture pieces—with art and accents used sparingly. Or, if you like a rich, warmer alternative, paint your walls in one of the handsome muted gold shades and pair with white accessories.

COLOR**OPTIONS**

LEFT: *For instant chic style, marry gold and white. Resist the temptation for all-gold accessories. Here, crystal vases are a lighter look for varying heights of fresh lilies and assorted greenery.*

RIGHT: *A painted floorcloth finishes a white-and-gold scheme in style and adds subtle pattern to the sleek room. As an alternative, consider a pale finish for a wood floor or off-white or palest gold carpet. Distressed gold finishes, such as this French-style armchair, give texture, rather than shine.*

COLOROPTIONS■

Beyond the glitter of gold, pair white with metallic shades of silver or pewter. Or try accents of cooler pinks for unexpected hints of color.

ABOVE: *Look to the traditional style of Early American houses for interesting ways to introduce color. Here, the chair rail and window trim imbue the dining room with color. The walls are a supporting tint. For interest and in keeping with the period style, the baseboard is painted slate black. To tie the spare look and subtle scheme together, the hanging corner cupboard repeats the green of the painted table.*

RIGHT: *One brightly painted piece of furniture can be all you need to jazz up a plain white room. Here, an old bed was simply painted with a fire engine shade of red enamel for a vibrant jolt of color. Use accents—the quilt and pillows—to tie such a contrasting scheme together and avoid a choppy look.*

COLOROPTIONS ■ *To make your touches count, choose a bold color—warm gold and pumpkin or cooler purple and teal.*

TOUCHES OF COLOR

When you are getting comfortable with more color in your home, think how to creatively introduce easy-to-live-with touches and accents. If you have been living with white or off-white walls and want to see how more color feels to you, reverse the standard of colorful walls and white trim. Instead, paint the chair rail or other woodwork in your color choice and use a pale, subtle tint of the same color for the walls. An easy method is to use the deepest, most intense shade on a paint chip for the trim and the palest tint on the same chip for the wall color. To get the most impact from your trim color, choose a semigloss paint for light-reflecting shine.

COLOROPTIONS

COLORQUICK!

Forget the paint can. When you are ready for instant and readily-available color, accent with just one or two bright accessories. Catalogues and home stores are chock-full of bright, moderately-priced pillows in patterns and solids. And, flea markets and craft shows yield colorful, affordable pieces. Even one or two touches have major impact against a noncolor scheme. Easiest of all, peruse your neighborhood grocery store, the farmer's market, and the flower shop for temporary touches. Save the colorful blue or green empties from bottled water. Vary sizes and shapes for interest. Or, brighten your rooms with blooming plants and fresh flowers. One bright flower, in mass, creates more color impact than a mixed bouquet.

RIGHT: *Think of a white kitchen and neutral upholstery as a canvas for your creativity. For the most impact, introduce the dynamics of primary colors. Here, red, yellow, and blue all play a part in energizing the scheme. Remember to repeat the colors so your palette looks planned, instead of random. For color without clutter, rotate and change accessories rather than adding to the mix. Alternative: Try prints and patterns in warmer yellow or softer green tones instead of blue and red.* **COLOROPTIONS■** *Give the primaries a twist by going beyond crayon box colors to orangy reds or lemony yellows paired with cobalt blue or vivid green. The trick for a harmonious look is to keep colors in the same intensity (degree of brightness). An easy way is to choose colors in the same place on the color chips.*

ABOVE: *Neutral and sophisticated, the comfortable living room mixes tailored cotton duck sofas with country-style pieces and folk art. Fill a favorite pottery piece with the brightest flowers you can find to make it come alive. In the early spring, try branches from flowering trees or in the fall, autumn foliage. When flowers are scarce, bowls of fruit are alternatives.*

RIGHT: *Color comes as easily as a grouping of pottery, vases, and plates. As you look for pieces, work with one strong hue, here the blue, to anchor and unify your scheme.*

WHOSE HUE TO USE?

Bored with beige? Feeling ennui with off-white walls? Don't be afraid to bring the power and personality of color into your home. Following a few simple guidelines, you can change the way you feel when you walk into a room and even how big that room looks. And, if you are confused by the rainbow of color choices, the following questions and answers will help you understand the power of color—and help put it to work for you.

Q *Can color change your mood from "blah" to "bouncy"?* Color creates a zone of feeling much like a "psychological thermostat." Red, orange, and yellow are sunny, energizing, even "hot" colors. They bring warmth and life to a room, stimulating conversation, appetites, and passion. On the other hand, blues, greens, and purples are cooling colors. They turn down the "heat," creating a calming and restful atmosphere.

Q *How do you set the "color temperature" throughout your home?* First, think of how the room will be used. Choose warm colors for lively and active areas, such as the kitchen or dining room. Cool colors are best suited for areas of rest and relaxation—the living room and bedrooms.

Consider the natural light and location of rooms as well. For a chilly room, or one with north-facing windows, use warm colors to bring a welcome coziness. Similarly, a south-facing room with blazing sunlight will benefit from cool colors that create a temperate climate.

Warm reds, oranges, and yellows draw walls in, making a large room seem cozier and more intimate. But cool blues, greens, and purples will make it appear larger. Use this power of color on walls and ceilings to change the space of your room without expensive construction.

Q *What colors are comfortable—and comforting— for you?* Color preference is intensely personal, often based on associations from your past and stimulated by everyday experiences. Choose colors that you associate with pleasant times and places. Think of colors that remind you of your favorite things: red rubies, green apples, sunny blue skies, purple sunsets.

Check out your clothing closet: it will give you a clear palette of the colors that make you happy every day. Stay away from the latest fads in colors—let your personal style shine through.

If you like to keep things light, pastel colors may be your best selections. They contain a lot of white, which reflects light, creating airy spaces. Use a cool pastel blue to make a room "grow" and appear restful, spacious, and calm.

Q *Do you want to keep things dark, deep, and dramatic?* Dark colors absorb light, creating intimate, cozy spaces. Use deep red, tobacco brown, coal black, and hunter green for dramatic passages, such as entryways, hallways, and stairways. Dark colors are also perfect choices for small rooms where you want to heighten the intimate atmosphere and for large rooms that have a lot of sunlight, windows, and doors.

Q *Can you use "plain shades" as mood makers?* Yes. Natural shades, such as gray, beige, taupe, and ivory, are actually neutral "uncolors" that rely on clever use of light and texture to create shadows for very atmospheric rooms. For interest, vary textures and materials, from smooth metals and warm woods to rough linens or burlaps.

Whites and ivories reflect light and bounce it off walls and surfaces to make a space feel bright and airy. Like green, these colors remind us of items found in nature, connecting us with the great outdoors.

Q *Can color give you a sensual "feeling" or change your environment?* Colors often evoke the sensory, tactile "feel" of different items. Shades of wheat, moss green, and mustard yellow recall earthy textures and natural objects and substances. "Jewel" colors—deep purple, deep red and gold—give the feeling of luxurious fabric textures and riches.

To quickly change the mood, choose neutral colors for your walls and upholstery and swap the colors of your pillows, area rugs, and lampshades to coordinate with the seasons: Use lively pinks and blues for summer; terra-cottas and gold for autumn; reds, blacks, and whites for winter; and shades of green for the coming of spring.

Q *Why choose paint to give your room a perfect "complexion"?* Wall paint is easy to use, quick, and usually the least expensive way to give a room an instant "makeover." Like cosmetics, it can mask less-than-perfect details and call attention to fine ones. Flat paint finishes are subdued compared to semigloss or gloss paints, which intensify colors.

Q *Can you use window dressings to jazz up your room color?* Window dressings are powerful color elements in a room, as the eye is drawn to the light of a window. Double the impact of your window dressings by lining them with a colored or patterned cloth and tying them back to expose the underside.

The type of lining is also important. If the lining is lightweight and light colored, drapery colors will intensify and glow as sunlight passes through them. A "black out" lining that is denser and heavier will literally block light and subdue (or deaden) the drapery colors.

Q *Can you get color impact from what's underfoot?* A floor carpeted in light solid color—the same as the wall color—will make a room grow. For the opposite effect, use area rugs (especially dark colors) to shrink the room by visually breaking up the floor space. Also, a highly polished wood floor reflects light.

Q *Do you notice what happens when you turn on the light?* Choose the right bulb for your room color. Incandescent bulbs will "warm" your room colors with a yellowish tone. It can make pale yellows practically disappear, some greens turn yellow green, and clay colors turn orange. Fluorescent lighting casts a bluish color—making reds turn deep raspberry and yellows into a greenish hue. (Color-corrected bulbs, without these effects, are available but expensive.)

Q *What colors can you use to give your home a vintage appearance?* Use "tea" colors that simulate aged materials. (These are colors that appear to be aged, the patina look of old fabrics and wallpaper.) You can even give new natural cotton or linen fabrics this look by dipping them in a tea bath of a tea-and-water solution.

Q *How can you plan a whole-house scheme? Should colors match exactly?* A total home scheme is just a larger version of a single room's color scheme. Consider the position of the rooms and their flow from one room to another. For easy transition, start with a color or two you like and vary the colors, accents, and intensities as you move from room to room. For a small home or a home with an open plan, paint the public rooms in one light color or tints of one color.

Often the most charming and successful interiors are those that offer colors in unusual combinations and off "matches." Perfectly matched colors can be dull and look too contrived.

Q *Can a bit of paint or accessories change a room when there's no time to do the walls?* For a big impact, paint the ceiling a color other than white. Or paint the fireplace a different color than your moldings; use a paint technique on a wood floor; paint the back of bookshelves or cupboards a different color than the front.

Inexpensive accessories can be the "jewelry" of a well-dressed room. Change your plain lampshades to colored ones or add a colorful fringe to the bottom of a plain shade. Display colorful collections of balls of yarn, glassware, or shells to give added spark without a lot of money.

Pink and Azure Blue

Lemon Yellow and Mint Green

Aquamarine and Sea Foam

Hyacinth and Lilac

Lime Green and Cobalt

Apricot and Peach

Tangerine and Melon

LIGHT
& BRIGHT

ENJOY A SUMMER MOOD ALL YEAR WITH A palette inspired by lighthearted pales or happy vibrant hues. To cool a climate with a long, hot summer, try a scheme based on the palest of pastels, as this bedroom at the beach illustrates. Generous touches of white keep the setting crisp, not sweet. Or, if brights are your style, experiment with some of the newest combinations that rev up shades of blues and greens or unexpected palettes into dynamic decorating. The fun of color is how easily you create a new look and set a personal mood with fresh backgrounds or just quick accents.

In a serene setting, use the merest hint of a pale tint for your wall color. Lighten a pretty pastel with white for a kiss of color. Here, the tint is seashell pink. For an unexpected twist, add a vibrant note such as the painted library ladder.

In today's no-boundaries schemes, think of white as half of a colorful decorating duo. If you enjoy an intense color, such as sunshine yellow, stripe your walls. The effect will be colorful but still airy. With clean white as the background, every accessory, from artwork to the tiniest teacup, stands out. Pastels are pretty, as soft shades are amplified by white.

PUNCH UP WHITE

LEFT: *Think of a pale interior as a neutral backdrop that's easy to change with accessories and art. Though the walls and upholstered pieces are light, the distinctive oil painting hung by a decorative rope sets a nautical theme. A watercolor, pottery, and floral fabrics could transform the room into cottage style, or sleek accessories could impart a contemporary spirit. For more on striping walls, see page 111.*

ABOVE: *Use a pale scheme as the ideal backdrop to mix furnishings and accessories.*

When you keep the walls, floors, and major pieces light, accessories, tableware, and linens take center stage. Distressed or color-washed pieces, such as this armoire used for storage, are ideal for touches of color that don't overpower the palette. Traditional country-finish cool blues and greens, in distressed finishes, work in pale rooms.

*COLOR**OPTIONS** ■ Yellow not you? Try greens, pinks, or periwinkle blue to stripe with white. Look for such alternative choices for every color scheme featured throughout this chapter.*

COLOR**OPTIONS**

COOL-DOWN COLORS

COLOROPTIONS ■ *Mixing a color with gray lowers the intensity. These accents add punch without heat; yellow, too, cools as a pale tint.*
ABOVE: *If you enjoy the pale coolness of pastels inside, consider the porch as an extension of the interior. Traditional clear-white trim provides a crisp contrast. Shutters and detailing stand out in more intense hues of compatible colors. Here, on a porch, teal green pairs naturally with pink and white.*

CENTER: *Tame the intense sun of a west-facing room with a refreshing pastel for the walls. Delightfully cool in summer, the scheme is equally pleasing in winter when the lower sun warms the room and the pale colors reflect precious winter light. When you frame large windows or French doors with a vibrant color, the outdoors becomes art. Light flooring, fabric, and furniture create a soothing scheme by minimizing contrast.*

Where the temperatures steam most of the year, residents naturally turn to the cool of pastels as a counterbalance to the sun. Today, the easy look of the tropics is a popular decorating style— even in much more temperate climates. To achieve this island-inspired palette, start with pale walls (pink and blue are traditional favorites) and paint the ceiling in an equally pale or slightly deeper tint. Blue and blue-green porch ceilings are traditional in the Caribbean and Florida Keys for relief from the heat and to protect homes from unfriendly spirits. (An easy way to achieve a pleasing color: Lighten the trim color from your paint chip.) In cooler climates, this lighthearted style translates well into sunrooms, porches, kitchens, or family rooms with western exposures. Or, follow tradition and paint your porch or sunroom ceiling icy blue.

RIGHT: *Searching for a wall color that flatters people and possessions? Pale pinks, which cast a soft rosy glow as they reflect both artificial and natural light, are ideal. Pink naturally works with equally pale blues, as in this sitting room/kitchen, or with yellows or greens of the same delicate intensity. In more formal settings, pink creates a delicate backdrop for dark wood furniture pieces, which benefit, as do people, from flattering light.*

Together, color and paint are the natural quick-change artists. Instantly, a fresh coat of paint revives a tired or dated interior and updates style. If you find a room too dark or closed in, change its personality with white, off-white, or the palest tint of a pastel. Light colors give a room a clean, new feel. And, light shades are famous for visually expanding small rooms. For an airy effect, paint woodwork and built-ins the same pale shade or a complementary light tint. Contrast between light and dark painted or stained wall finishes will chop up a room so it feels smaller. With proper preparation (see page 111) dark stained paneling can be painted. If your drywall is in good condition, choose paint with some sheen to reflect light. Eggshell and satin finishes are options. If you like more shine and light reflection and an easy-to-clean surface, try a semigloss finish.

FRESHEN UP

LEFT: *White paint instantly refreshes a once-dark-paneled casual dining area. Note the hanging cupboard and even the wide mat for the watercolor are white. For interest, vary textures when one pale dominates. Here, the cupboard has been distressed with a light sanding for a stylish, casual country accent.*

ABOVE: *Use a white background when you want furnishings and art to take center stage. Here, the simple white shelves display collected folk art, and the checkerboard painted coffee table adds a lighthearted grid motif. Use such touches of black and darker art to impart a sophisticated edge to a light scheme. The mask and folk art pieces unify the wall between the chest and the oil painting.*

RIGHT: *Paint a furniture piece bright white and experiment with fun accents. To keep it simple, choose such motifs as the pastel stripes, the freehand checkerboard trim, and the polka dots. Use enamels or seal latex paint with polyurethane. Add pulls, in fun shapes, to update the look.*

COLOROPTIONS *Add touches of pretty colors to white schemes for freshness. Medium blues, greens, yellows, or pinks are good choices.*

If you love a color combination, enjoy it as the star of a room scheme. When blues and greens are your thing, go beyond pale greens to acid shades. Housewares sections of department or home stores are great places to see what's out there as the colors are fun for casual linens and accessories. You'll see variations of bright, clear lime green and paler, yellower tints. The joy of these greens is that they work well together and play off their classic blue partners. Cobalt blue, here and on page 51, pairs with these greens. Or try sky blue. Accent colors of melon, terra-cotta, and clear, sunny yellow are pleasing with this duo. For whole rooms, the strong blue works best as the accent unless you want a dark, dramatic wall color. Repeat the blue in other elements to tie the scheme together. Not ready for such a jolt? Paint trim a soft green and use cobalt accessories.

FOCUS ON COLOR

OPPOSITE: *Based on Mediterranean colors, the drama comes from the bold use of intense blue and bright yellow green. Trim is painted in gloss enamel to heighten the dramatic effect.*

RIGHT: *Find a fabric or table linen that has the greens and blues you like and have the paint mixed to match. You'll already have shades chosen to work together. If you like a country casual look, shop for a check or plaid based on the blue-green combination. Or, try blue, green, and yellow.*

COLOROPTIONS ■

Need ideas? Choose a pair or a threesome based on these sophisticated, lively shades of blue and green.

COLOROPTIONS

BUILDING BLOCKS

Used creatively, color works as building blocks—visually creating structure. Imagine this inviting, cheerful kitchen as an all-white or light gray space. Would you notice the open shelves across the window, the island's gentle curve, or how it's trimmed below? Want to call attention to a design feature? Paint it a strong or arresting color. Want to de-emphasize an element? Use a cool or neutral color; it recedes into the background. Effective use of color means thinking beyond the expected. Contemporary-style kitchens are often white or black and white. But here, melon warms the cool gray and off-white walls. The combination is fresh without being fussy, colorful without dominating.

RIGHT: *Consider the overall effect of color choices. The contemporary, ceiling-hung shelves and island are strong design elements as they stand out against the pale walls. Matching walls would have overpowered the small space, and an all-neutral kitchen would have lacked the vibrancy and design punch. Pair such a warm color with a cool hue—here gray—for the excitement of contrast.*

COLOROPTIONS■

For more design-building colors, choose two or more of these easy-to-live-with, 1950s-inspired hues.

COLOROPTIONS

BELOW: *Remember every element in a design can't be the star. When you use colorful laminates, choose restful neutrals for walls and flooring. Or, if you like the idea of easy-to-change schemes, paint your walls in two colorful shades, and switch to neutral laminates for countertops.*

ABOVE: *Laminates are limited no more. Today you can find virtually any color or color variation of the popular cladding material. In a kitchen, darker laminates are easier to maintain in areas that get heavy everyday use. Use lighter or brighter laminates for more decorative surfaces. With today's technology, you can easily match trim color to a laminate or choose a blending shade.*

LIGHT & BRIGHT

Working with color is part art and part science, but there are some givens that make it a little easier. You'll often hear the terms "value" and "intensity" used in referring to color. Value simply means how light or dark the color is. Blue, for example, can be very pale pastel—a light value—or midnight—a dark value. Intensity means how clear or bright the color is. What can be confusing is that pastels (light values of colors) can also be bright. Hot pink may be pink, but it's certainly vivid. There are no right or no wrong color or value mixes. But when you choose colors of the same value and intensity, the effect

is naturally harmonious. If you want your overall effect to be light and airy, without the drama of sharp contrast, choose equally pale shades of the dominant colors you are using. Pair a pale shell pink, for example, with a delicate apple green rather than a jewel tone forest green. Or, if you lean to brights, plan your main scheme so the colors balance each other. In the bedroom, above right, the buttery yellow is intense and bright enough to visually hold its own with the deep, vibrant red. Repeat colors, shown in the mix of fabric patterns, tie two strong hues together.

LEFT: *Pretty pale schemes work because tints of delicate color amplify rather than compete with each other. To avoid starkness, use a pastel tint, such as this pale apple green, rather than white, for the walls. Pale pink is another shade that flatters, too, without dominating the scheme. Fabrics of the same value in this pretty setting feature light, open backgrounds for floral prints. To keep the accessories light, blue-and-white porcelains are a natural choice.*

ABOVE: *There's no halfway with bold, intense schemes. This vibrant red bedroom is visually pleasing because the yellow-and-red print fabrics are vivid and intense. The yellow, the second major color, is equally as strong as the red. Such bold schemes also work by repetition; the red is repeated in the mix of prints. White and black and wood tones provide the needed relief from the jolts of two strong, vivid colors.*

WHEN YOU DESIRE CALM, LIMIT color for a soothing environment without the visual excitement of bright shades or vivid patterns. Neutrals usually refer to the "noncolors" shown here with black as an accent. Monochromatic schemes are variations of one color, which may or may not be neutral. Neutrals create interest in their own right, relying on texture and subtle variation, rather than the instant impact of color. Light accent colors are often part of the scheme.

Ice Blue and Warm Gray

French Vanilla and Almond

Pale Blue and Blush

Terra–Cotta and Sable

Honey Wheat and Olive

Metallics and Ochre

Cool Gray and Barely Beige

RESTFUL
NEUTRALS

Sophisticated and soothing, this bedroom employs a mix of subtle patterns, fabrics, and furnishings for interest. Use painted and distressed finishes as well as informal accessories, such as the quilt, to relax formal furnishings and monochromatic schemes.

SETTING A CONTEMPORARY MOOD

COLOR**OPTIONS**

The essence of contemporary is strong design and clean lines—a philosophy that naturally lends itself to a limited palette of white, black, and neutrals, sometimes with vivid accent colors. As every element of the room is integral to the design, choose shades and finishes for walls and floors that create a gallery-like background for furniture, art, and carefully-chosen accessories. Shades of white, the classic noncolors, often pair with natural wood and metal pieces as well. Consider art when choosing wall colors. White walls are often the choice for contemporary art and photography, but some designers like richly colored oil paintings against warmer sand shades.

COLOR*OPTIONS* ■ *Enliven contemporary black and white with a jolt of bold color—beyond clear red, consider the saturated shades of leaf green, warm gray, cranberry, or coppery brown.*
ABOVE: *With a white beginning, introduce subtle color variations with Berber carpet. Note the mix of textures from the chrome-and-leather chair to the parchment lampshade. Touches of black—the gallery-type frame and the chest hardware—add weight to a pale setting.*
LEFT: *Contemporary soothes when the setting is as clean and pristine as this all-white living room, enlivened by the grid of black-framed engravings. The silk pillow fabric alludes to the finish of the metal tea cart used as a coffee table.*
OPPOSITE: *No pattern is needed in a contemporary apartment where white and glass walls allow the ever-changing city scene to be the most arresting element. The brick-red-and-black chair and metal footed table, modern furniture classics, appear to be in a gallery setting.*

HINTS OF COLOR

Using tints, colors lightened by white, is the perfect way to add hints of pale color to neutral schemes. To keep the softness and serenity of neutrals, introduce only tints of one pale color paired with your neutrals. Cool colors—the pale blues and lavenders here—are ideal, as they are naturally serene, calm, passive colors. In such a scheme, the whites should be equally soft and muted; bright white would be a jarring contrast. Fabrics should mix pale color with white or off-white; avoid solid blocks of all but the palest of pales. If you prefer a warmer shade, such as shell pink, opt for the palest tint.

COLOR**OPTIONS**

COLOR**OPTIONS** ■

Look to the tints of always-flattering, pretty pink—when you are introducing barely-there accents. For the softest look, use the lightest tint for the walls and repeat in small, more colorful... doses around the room.

LEFT: *Even with traditional furnishings, an all-white room feels austere. Here, the mood is still cool and calm but with the hints of pale lavender and subtle florals. (Note the white background and delicate framing for the botanical prints.) Be equally careful how you add accessories. In this bedroom, mirrored glass, silver, and crystal vary the textures and surfaces without undue color competition. The palest roses are the final finishing touch.*

LEFT: *Natural pine adds texture and warmth without overpowering pale tints. When you want to introduce a color—here a blue upholstered chair—repeat it in smaller accents such as the stenciled oars on the armoire and the quilt, to avoid a spotty effect. Note the caned chair, once dark, has more contemporary life, courtesy of white paint and recovered cushions. Even in a light setting, a touch of black (lampshade, candles) adds an extra hint of style.*

ABOVE: *When you restrict color to white and a pale tint, consider uniting the scheme by combining both as a painted floor or rug. Remember, too, that when color is subtle, you'll want to carefully choose shapes, fabrics, and finishes. Here, note the repetition of the oval shape for the side cabinet, the table at the foot of the bed, and the dresser mirror. The mix of the cotton print draperies, cutwork table skirt, and quilt adds variations of scale and pattern.*

WHEN TEXTURES ENLIVEN

By common decorating definition, neutral schemes tend to be in the natural shades of off-whites, creams, beiges, and pale taupes. These colors are close enough on the color wheel that it's fair to consider them monochromatic palettes. It comes down to this in decorating. How do you get the soothing quality of a neutral, basically one-color or no-color scheme and avoid boredom? When color isn't the key player, you use shapes, textures, and carefully chosen patterns for warmth and interest.

Start out easy. Think of your room with neutral walls and major furniture as your first decorating step. Begin easy with lamp bases in different materials—such as natur-al wood and pottery. Nothing jarring, just different. Use the same approach with window treatments, table skirts, throws, or accent pillows. Vary the shapes, sizes, fabrics, and trims on accent pillows. Consider how accessories fit into the overall scheme without overpowering. Glass, crystal, distressed tin, pottery, wood, even concrete garden ornaments all introduce texture without color and pattern. Use architectural fragments, such as windows or gates, or subdued prints or etchings rather than bright paintings. Mix the smooth with the rough, the rustic and the refined—such as unglazed terra-cotta and a crystal vase—for most interest.

OPPOSITE: *Textures— note the three wood tables—and subtle patterns bring life and style to a coolly neutral living room. The botanical print blends while a bright painting would be jarring.*

RIGHT: *Well-chosen accessories infuse a neutral scheme with spirit. Touches of gold in the wall sculpture and frame balance the plank table and concrete ornaments. Tiny details— piping on chairs and pillow trim—contribute to design. Add plants, flowers, and fruit to make a neutral room come alive.*

COLOR TRENDS COME AND GO, BUT CLASSIC combinations, just like classic-style clothing, are always in fashion. Whether you lean to the contemporary or the traditional, you'll find time-honored color schemes that work with your own look. Ever-crisp blue and white or always-stylish black and white are natural choices for interiors from the most contemporary architectural rooms to the most traditional bedrooms or sun porches. Add bright accents of red or yellow, and you'll have lively schemes that adapt to a variety of styles and decorating moods. When your goal is to warm up a room, turn to the appealing soft yellows, heated up by vibrant reds. Or, when drama is your goal, consider the enduring power of red or the sophistication of jewel tones to create rooms with instant presence. Classics cool down, too. Beyond beloved blues, plan rooms based on the natural charm of shades of restful green or friendly yellows and greens.

Blue and White

Blue, White, and Yellow

Red, White, and Blue

Black and White and...

Red Plus Red

Sunshine Yellows

Shades Of Green

The Jewel Tones

CLASSIC PALETTES

Think of the classic white kitchen as a blank canvas for decorating creativity. Start with quick-change and easy-to-find blue-and-white accents in plates and linens; add red or other equally-vibrant flowers for lively fun.

Start with black and white and you'll develop a scheme that's as versatile as it is tasteful and ever stylish. Strong in its own right, the neutral noncolor scheme gracefully accepts a vivid third element. When you want a strong statement, add color for walls as the foyer illustrates. Or, keep the scheme easily changeable with smaller shots of pure color. Be sure to choose a hue bold enough to partner with this graphic pair.

BLACK
& WHITE AND...

OPPOSITE: *Mix fabric patterns and vary the scale or print to take advantage of the design possibilities of black and white. Toile, the French-inspired scenic print used for this bed hanging, is a natural to combine with the stripes, checks, and diamond patterns shown here. Note the woven carpet adds another pattern to heighten design interest. The judicious use of clear red accents brings the limited palette to life.*

LEFT: *Perfect for this traditional entry hall or a more contemporary setting, the deep burgundy red enlivens the classic black-and-white tile floor and crisp white woodwork. Touches of brass and gilded framing add sparkle to the setting. Variations of red are natural with black and white, as the hot hue warms what can be a cool scheme.*

COLOROPTIONS ■ *Balance the strong graphic quality of black and white with a clear, intense color.*

COLOR **OPTIONS**

BLUE & WHITE

From the classic 18th-century Chinese export porcelains to the pretty French cotton scenic toiles to crisp awning stripes, no color combination is more beloved than blue and white. Though clear medium and deeper blues are often paired with tints of whites and off-whites, the shades of blue are as endless as the sky. From the intensity of midnight and cobalt blue to the delicacy of the palest, coolest tint, you can find the perfect shade or shades of this always-favorite color. For fun, mix several shades of blue or different patterns, such as combinations of toiles, checks, stripes, prints, plaids, and florals. To avoid visual overload, choose only one dominant print or floral and let the other patterns be supporting players. Mix in porcelain and pottery pieces and you'll have a scheme as easy as it is stylish.

COLOR **OPTIONS**

OPPOSITE LEFT: *Tailored, yet lighthearted, stripes translate well into multifunctions, such as this padded window lambrequin and window seat cushion. Notice how the block-print style floral pillow, in the same size as the striped pillow, and the casual combination of blue-and-white accessories bring the scheme to life.*

TOP CENTER: *Be bold with blue and use a dark background wallpaper to*

dramatically decorate a master bath. Note the pleasing effect of matching the wallpaper to the window treatment fabric and stenciling the white cabinets in a complementary motif. Blue willow-pattern plates, on stands, are always right for this classic motif and color combination.

LEFT: *In a bedroom with graceful French-style furniture, use a detailed blue-and-white cotton print to add warmth and softness. The dust ruffle is a stripe, but*

a matching fabric would be pleasing, too. Note how the Chinese motif porcelain lamp enhances the carefully edited color palette.

ABOVE: *When you want to keep your scheme on the light side, choose an open, white background print to showcase blue motifs. Restrict your scheme to one cotton or linen print, here a toile style, to keep the look cool and calm.*

COLOROPTIONS ■ *From sky to sea to a baby's eyes, blues are everywhere.*

BLUE & WHITE & YELLOW

Classic for spring gardens and for decorating, blue and yellow pair two popular primaries into one of the prettiest, freshest combinations. Almost opposites on the color wheel (see page 19), they create the excitement of opposite attraction. Deep blues and vibrant yellows set a dramatic tone in a living or formal dining room. Or, in paler tints, blues and yellows are perfect for kitchens, family rooms, bedrooms, nurseries, or porches. Again, depending on your furnishings and accessories, the look can easily range from European to American Country to contemporary. To warm up this scheme, paint the walls a soft sunshine, butter, or mustard yellow. Or, for a cooler, more restful look, perfect for a bedroom, choose a pale blue for your walls and accent with white.

ABOVE: *Blue and white warm against sunshine-yellow walls. When gently distressed pieces are the focal points, choose a delicate shade that won't compete with your antiquing finds.*

TOP RIGHT: *Love blue and yellow? Want a sophisticated and versatile look? Play dark blue and bright yellow fabrics, covering classic furnishings, against a neutral sofa and creamy walls and window treatments. Choose a dark rug to anchor the scheme and balance the airy backdrop. Add blue accent accessories. With this refreshed look, your favorites sing a jazzy new tune.*

BOTTOM RIGHT: *Collectors of blue-and-white porcelains and pottery, especially the blue willow pattern, are a legion. These favorites shine against a background of lemon or butter yellow. Painted the same lemon yellow as the dining room, the entry and stairwell extend the happy color. Lovers of blue and yellow often expand their collecting, mixing yellow and blue-and-yellow pieces with their blue and white. The more the merrier works here.*

COLOROPTIONS ■ *From palest straw to rich wheat gold, shades of yellow are the happiest partners for beloved blues.*

MOODS OF BLUE

From the sleekest contemporary to the coziest Colonial, blue works in your decorating scheme. Cool and restful, blue is associated visually and aesthetically with peace and serenity. Think of the sea and the outdoors and the expanse of the sky. Light tints of blue open up a room, keeping the feel airy and summer fresh. (Tint the ceiling paint, too, for just a hint of coolness.) Dark, intense blues, such as cobalt or royal, give a room weight and drama. Beyond the walls, window treatments in rich brocades and velvets have traditionally been blue, trimmed with gold. Or, follow the example of nature and mix blues for a room that sings a gentle song. Use pale blue for your walls and darker, grayed blue for trim. Or, mix grayed blues with clear medium and dark navy blues. When you are not sure of what blue to use, pick out a paint chip and try swatches of the lightest and darkest shades. To quickly warm a blue scheme, introduce green, yellow, or red accents.

OPPOSITE: *With easy style, shades of blue create a restful, simple bedroom. Go beyond walls to doors and ceiling to surround yourself with the blues of sea, sky, and summer flowers.*

ABOVE LEFT: *Employ blue to emphasize, but not overshadow, architecture in a contemporary setting. Here, the blue niche effectively "frames" a white-matted print.*

ABOVE RIGHT: *Classic Colonial blue, often seen in 18th-century-style interiors, gives the appropriate backdrop for a collection of pewter pieces. Seasonal yellow daffodils seem to pop to life against the darker background.*

COLOROPTIONS ■ *There's a blue for any taste. Intense cobalt blues to pale tropical shades to fun turquoises.*

RIGHT: *You don't have to paint your walls fire engine red to enjoy the romance of a red room. Instead, use a fabric such as this scenic toile print, which offers the relief of a white background. For most impact, use enough fabric to make a statement—here the bed hanging, coverlet, and window treatment unify the design.*

BELOW: *Brick red warms rooms with dark-painted or stained wood as this kitchen illustrates. In a room with high ceilings and stainless steel, red makes what could be a cold space into a room that's inviting. Not sure of your shade? Paint three swatches on the wall and note how light affects intensity.*

RED!

No other color carries the symbolism of power and glory that red does. Long associated with royalty and celebrations, red connotes energy, excitement, passion, and warmth. Use large doses of red in active, vibrant rooms such as a nighttime dining room or a kitchen for family gatherings. Or cozy up a study or library with a dark, rich shade. Reds range from the cooler purple (burgundy) side of the spectrum to clear, pure brights to warmer brick and lively orange-tinged shades. If too much red overpowers, lighten with white or grayed neutrals for airiness without color competition. As an alternative, consider key decorative accents such as pillows, throws, or lamp shades.

ABOVE: *Use the strength of red to establish your design. Here the exterior red door, painted in shiny enamel, hints at the reds to come. Note how the red-white-and-blue-plaid foyer chair sets the stage for the red-and-white dining room visible through the cased opening.*

RIGHT: *Known as the color that increases appetite, red is a natural for the dining room. For spark and spunk, choose a semigloss red or apply an extra top layer of shiny glaze.*

COLOR OPTIONS ■

From bricks and oranges to cranberries and deep royal purplish hues, reds enliven.

COLOR **OPTIONS**

SUNSHINE YELLOWS

ABOVE LEFT: *For color without claustrophobia, paint a small, windowless powder room in a buttery shade. The background creates a soft glow for sconces and pretty floral fabrics often used in such dressy settings. If your walls are in good condition, choose paint with a semigloss finish for the pleasant effect of shine and for light reflection.*

ABOVE RIGHT: *Though pale and airy, the lightest tints of yellow warm a traditional-style dining room without intense color. With just a hint of pale color, this yellow allows the antique chairs and painted pedestal table to be the focal points. Note the subtle contrast between the white table and the pale sunlight of the walls. A more vibrant shade would create a jarring contrast not as visually pleasing and not as easy to live with. Such a subtle yellow tint provides a soft backdrop for delicate prints, art and plates as well as silver and china.*

Classic for kitchens and nurseries, yellow has good cheer that enlivens formal living and dining rooms as effectively. No room, from the most casual to the most formal, is immune to the power of this happiest color. Reputed to lift spirits, yellow gives the glow of the sun to dark, cheerless spaces and stands up to the color-draining powers of a wall of windows on a western exposure. With the ever-increasing paint choices, you'll easily find the palest tints perfect for porches, nurseries, and sunrooms to clear yellows to shades of mustard popular for Country French-inspired rooms. To let your favored yellow shine, pair it with white trim and woodwork.

ABOVE: *Often considered a neutral, bright, sunny yellow balances vibrant reds, blues, and greens. Here, a pretty medium shade holds it own with the classic red floral and deep-hued, patterned rug—and is a handsome backdrop for the black sconce shades above the mantel and the mix of collected accessories and framed art.*

ABOVE RIGHT: *If you love yellow, live with it. In black and white, this kitchen would have been handsome, but when the cabinets were painted a clear butter yellow, it sang. Such a jolt of unexpected color adds personality to your decorating. The yellow doesn't overpower as the cabinets feature glass doors instead of solid expanses of eye-level color.*

COLOROPTIONS *Think of pale yellows and yellow greens as the delicate colors of early spring that warm the cold earth with the first hints of color. These shades of cheer will likewise warm your home and heart through the year.*

ABOVE: *Forest green wall covering sets a restful mood in a master or guest bedroom. The deep background showcases framed botanical prints. Repeat such strong color as accent—here the lamp-shade and as greens in floral print—for continuity.*

RIGHT: *Create a cozy retreat by darkening the walls of a room with high ceilings and tall windows. Blues of this hue give instant intensity without overpowering with a bright, vivid shade. Repeat the shade as the fabric background for a harmonious feel. When walls are in good condition, use satin or semigloss paint for nighttime shine and depth.*

OPPOSITE: *A little can go a long way with deep colors. Enrich a neutral scheme by adding or recovering a pair of club chairs. (Or, even try a ready-made seasonal slipcover.) Enhance with generously scaled accent pillows for color continuity.*

COLOROPTIONS ■ *Think of the royal robes of purple and blue, studded crowns of precious stones, deep hues that shimmer and shine. With jewel tones, the depth of color imparts the richness.*

JEWEL BOX RICHES

Deep, saturated colors soak in the light, making a large room instantly cozier or a room with a cool exposure instantly richer. Jewel tones—ruby reds, deep emerald greens, sapphire blues, amethyst purples—create drama for living and dining rooms. Lit by chandeliers, soft lamp light, and the glow of candles, these colors sparkle and shimmer in contrast to the night outside. In today's decorating, the deep hues are used, too, in smaller rooms, such as cozy bedrooms or sitting rooms. Or, use jewel accents for neutral interiors or as warmth-creating seasonal changes. Pick out pillows and a throw in one or more of your favored hues. Add glass accessories or lampshades for chic, deep-toned touches.

ADD PATTERN TO PALETTES

Express your color personality with lively combinations that suit both your decorating mood and your style. For a quick start, begin with a focal-point fabric that has all the colors you plan to use. Then add at least two more patterns in varying scales. For harmony, repeat at least one of the colors from your focal-point fabric in the supporting fabrics or wall covering. Or, for a more subtle mix, consider smaller scale fabrics that blend without repeating colors as the more formal example illustrates. The idea is for the shades and patterns to gently complement each other, without a dominant fabric. (Colors of the same brightness are easiest to mix.)

OPPOSITE: *With blue and red as the repeating colors, stripes mix pleasantly with a floral cotton and a two-color quilt. Employ accents, such as the checkerboard, to introduce another pattern and texture. For more pattern, add a blue-and-white plaid or red-white-and-blue plaid fabric.*

RIGHT: *Subtle mixes of pattern give interest without vivid color or large scale. Use the walls, here pale yellow-and-white painted stripes, to introduce pattern. When colors are as subdued as these, they are considered neutral and don't have to be repeated. Notice repetition of gold in the Greek key border and the gilded details on the painted chair. The seat fabric is a fleur-de-lis, used as a repeating geometric pattern. The sage green of the upholstered chair blends with the soft red, as the colors are of equal intensity.*

YOUR COLOR CHOICES DON'T COME in right or wrong answers. If you decorate with colors you love, you'll create a warm, comforting haven from the cares of the world. The trick comes from choosing the most appealing shades and tints and mixes and matches of favorites. Here, three personal color palettes—of soft pastels, vibrant primaries, and stylish neutrals—illustrate the power and charming grace of color.

SUCCESS STORIES

Yellow and Gray With Accent;

Touches of Red and Florals;

Patchwork Primaries Nestled

With Natural Wood;

Creamy Whites, Taupes, and

Grays With Fabric Accents

in Graphic Prints of Black

and Sandalwood.

Your color choices extend above the four walls. Here, to incorporate two favorite colors, the boxed-beam ceiling is painted aqua and detailed with narrow bands of deep and pale peach. The aqua ceiling tint cools the warmth of a peach wallcovering.

Color, color everywhere literally floods this rambling house, where three generations gather to visit and relax. Taking cues from the nearby sea and sun and the owners' love of English style, the open rooms are filled with pretty, clear shades ranging from the pastel to the vibrant. The living room, pictured here, showcases two favorites: Walls papered in a flattering, glowing peach and the box-beam ceiling painted aqua and peach. Starting with colors that make you happy is an ideal way to begin your palette—whether you are decorating a whole house or a room or two. For a conventional ceiling, choose a tint of one of your favorite colors, an easy way to add another shade to your scheme. White trim is an effective relief and soothing counterpoint to such happy, colorful spaces.

HAPPY COLORS EVERY DAY

ABOVE: *With pretty tints of peach and accents of blue and green, this floral sofa fabric provides an inspired start for a living area and stair hall's color scheme. Carefully consider your shade when you are painting such an open arrangement of space. Wall color varies and changes in a room with large windows on two sides. Try test swatches in several different areas to find just the shade that looks best.*

LEFT: *Painted beams, aqua detailed with two shades of peach, visually lower a ceiling and create a feeling of coziness. Note the aqua and tints of blue are repeated in fabrics, as is the peach, effectively tying the scheme together. Peach used here, as well as shades of pink, is ideal for living areas, as the reflected light is flattering to dark woods and, more importantly, to people.*

HAPPY COLORS EVERY DAY

ABOVE: *To enjoy your favorite colors, think of the flow from room to room throughout your home. Colors should blend but not necessarily repeat. Here the library cocoons in the warmth of clear red, repeated in the floral fabric and accent pillows. The color also gives transition between bedrooms with blue walls and an English-style wallpaper. Note the white shelves alleviate color overload.*

RIGHT: *Where a forest green kitchen could be dark, green-and-white awning stripes are just right for a colorfully crisp backdrop. The green, relieved by white trim, repeats as the handsome tiles for the backsplash and counter.*

ABOVE: *Orangy yellow and cobalt blue are opposites on the color wheel, which means that together, they create a dynamic scheme with snap and style. Here, the lively look, based on an 18th century toile de Jouy fabric (French scenic design), enlivens a guest bedroom where iron bedsteads are painted to match. The power of the design comes from judicious repetition. As toiles are typically printed as fabrics and wallcoverings, they are ideal for schemes that call for window treatments and for wallcovering. Or, if you like the impact of this color pairing but prefer a simpler look, paint the walls in the warm yellow and use the toile only as fabric. Painted furniture adds another dimension to your color scheme and is an effective technique to repeat a color. Consider the supporting players, such as blue-and-white quilts. Unified rooms depend on controlling your palette through repeating accents, rather than introducing tiny bits of unrelated colors.* **COLOROPTIONS ■** *For a soft look, create a palette with clear, spring-fresh pastels, such as minty green, sky blue, sunshine yellow, and rosy pink.*

CREATING A FAMILY HAVEN

Planned for good times and lots of family fun, this color-splashed north woods lake house exudes warmth and cheer. The fun starts in the anything-but-formal dining room, where vivid, ever-upbeat red pairs with bright white. The green chairs, with red plaid seats, erase any doubts that infomality and easy comforts are the order of

the day. Most playful of all is the kitchen where cabinets, painted as folk art, repeat the dining room's red, white, and green and introduce blue and yellow into the lighthearted primary scheme. Remember all rooms in a home don't have to be equally colorful. Here the pale living room affords relief and allows the dining room to take color charge. When you plan colors for a weekend home or a year-round, much-used family room or kitchen, consider setting and orientation. This lake house, used in winter as well as summer, comes to life with warm colors and mixed patterns. If you live in a hot climate, or if you are painting a room with a sunny, western exposure, think of sherbet shades, such as pale lemon. The effect is lighthearted, yet refreshing.

ABOVE: A classic for dining rooms, red takes a playful twist when paired with painted green chairs. This opposite attraction, repeated in the plaid chair fabric, instantly enlivens a decorating scheme. When you use an intense wall color, such as red, remember the importance of white to balance. Here, the red appears even more vibrant and appealing above the white wainscoting and chair rail.

RIGHT: Try two colors for upper and lower cabinets, but don't stop there. The fun of this kitchen comes from the childlike motifs painted freehand in a popular primary palette with black accents.

ABOVE: *Before deciding on your color emphasis, consider a room's assets, here the living room's stone fireplace and beadboard walls. With the stonework as the natural focal point, walls and furniture stay light and neutral. Color comes from the crisp chair cushions, which can be changed seasonally for a warmer, cozier look. In summer, the flag pillows are perfect for the festive and patriotic classic red, white, and blue palette.*
COLOROPTIONS ■ *For the drama of red but with a cooler feel, try mossy greens, rusty oranges, or deep teal. Interchange these arresting shades to tailor a palette that will enliven your living and dining rooms with a stylish backdrop.*

EASY-TO-LIVE WITH NEUTRALS

Pale color quietens and soothes a combination living room/study, melding an array of patterns and decorative elements into a calming retreat. Begin with the background of gently ragged sandstone-colored walls. (For a quick faux paint technique, see page 111.) This soft, washed color and subtle texture warm the room without the jolt of strong color, patterned wallpaper, or the starkness of white. The sandstone effect also creates an appropriately nature-inspired backdrop for a room filled with faux animal prints, batik print fabrics, tropical rattan, and artifacts from overseas travels. In contrast, the painted floor provides a striking but decidedly neutral counterpoint—just the opposite effect of a heavily patterned rug. The simple motif also works well with the choice of the faux jungle animal print for the sofa. When one element in a room is this striking in color contrast, simplify the others to avoid overwhelming. Because of the detail of the stylized design, a decorative painter designed and executed the motif over a previously painted floor. (As a budget stretcher, consider a painted floorcloth or contact a local high school, art school or college for student painters or instructors who do freelance projects.)

Effective use of color, as this room so handsomely illustrates, means knowing when to stop and opt for none. Key to the success is the effective use of crisp white for the ceiling and woodwork, including the mantel. Equally striking would be white walls and woodwork with the mantel in a warm sand shade.

BELOW: *Though this room features a faux jungle animal print sofa, the palette emulates earthy shades of the natural environment. For a calming mood, the other colors and textures harmoniously support, not compete with the lively animal print focal point. To keep this room neutral, walls are ragged in a sandstone shade—visual balance without a heavy dose of color. And floors are painted in a light cream, then treated to a stylized medallion. Likewise, the white painted trim and bookcases and white chair contribute to the airiness. The architectural frieze is art without the color of a painting. In a scheme like this, accents of bright or jewel tones would be jarring to the natural colors and textures. The gold picture frames add just a touch of sparkle—as gold jewelry does to a tailored suit.*

OPPOSITE: *At the opposite end of the sitting room/study, a mirror reflects light and wall color for maximum impact of the pleasing sandstone. Note the mix of textures, which gives interest and support without competing with the animal print. Note, too, how a black accent, here the lacquered-and-gilded armchair, easily brings a chic edge to a room setting. One easy-to-do design rule: Almost any room can benefit from just a touch of black. Vary the amounts of black to achieve the contrasts you want. For shine, introduce black-lacquer finishes.*

COLOROPTIONS■ *The yellow undertones of sandstone not your look? Try grayed or light stone or pewter ragged walls, paired with white, for an equally neutral background for round-the-world collectibles.*

COLOR

PAINT AND THE BASICS OF COLOR.

If you know what color or colors of paint you want to use in a room, great. With today's technology, paint stores can mix and tint to match whatever shade you love. Just about anything works—a swatch of fabric, a piece of porcelain, artwork, a photograph, even a chambray shirt.

INSTANT COLOR

Checkerboard Patterns

Striped Walls

Painted Paneling

Sponging Techniques

Faux Tiled Walls

When you haven't decided on the shade you want, start with three to five samples of paint chips in your color range. (More than five is generally confusing.) Some companies today offer oversize chips, which are easier to see than the smaller, multishade cards. Tack up the chips and observe the colors at different times of day and with artificial and natural light. When you have two or three shades that work, buy a pint of each and paint a wallboard scrap or wall section in your choice. If your room has varying light conditions, such as a wall of windows or French doors, paint sections in two or more spots to be sure you are happy with your choice. (See page 14 for details.) It's easy for even an experienced decorator to be fooled by the effects of light, floor coverings, and furnishings on paint colors. So unless you are absolutely certain of your choice, don't skip this step.

Remember, too, that the finish of the paint—flat, satin, eggshell, semigloss, or gloss—will affect the light-reflecting qualities and the ultimate color. What finish you choose is a personal preference, although flat paint is generally preferred for less-than-perfect walls. Paint with some shine, such as satin or even shinier semigloss, is also used in kitchens, baths, or children's rooms, as it's easier to scrub. Again, depending on your preference, you might like the light-reflecting qualities of semigloss paint for a dramatic dining room used at night or even a small decorative powder room. Semigloss is used for woodwork and trim, but follow your taste.

• **Caution:** White and off-whites are at least as tricky as vivid colors. **One final tip**: *If you love a color, but it's overpowering, switch to a lighter value of the same paint chip. It's also possible to get the paint store to custom mix a shade between two adjacent values on the paint chip.*

HOW MUCH PAINT TO BUY?

Paint cans usually state the one-coat coverage you can expect from 1 gallon of paint or primer. For many paints, including primers, a gallon will cover about 400 square feet. But it's still a good idea to calculate coverage. Measure the perimeter of the room (all walls). Multiply the result by the ceiling height to get the square footage. Round off to the full foot. Don't deduct for windows or other openings unless they add up to more than 100 square feet. Divide that figure into the number of square feet that a gallon of paint promises to cover. Round up to the nearest whole number. Buy accurately, as it is difficult to match paint if you need more or to dispose of properly if you buy too much. However, it's always a good idea to save paint for touch-ups, especially if you think you may rearrange artwork or rehang window hardware.

WHAT OTHER SUPPLIES DO I NEED?

The tools are simple but necessary for interior painting. Here's what you will need for the basic paint jobs:

• *Primer*

• *Brown paper drop cloths for the floor; heavy plastic drop cloths for furniture*
• *Surfacing compound and knife to apply it, sandpaper, painter's tape, edger*
• *Metal paint pan, plastic liners, roller with threaded handle for extensions, sash and trim brushes. Most interior jobs call for a 7- or 9-inch roller frame. Use a long pole for the ceiling and a short pole (2 feet long) for walls.*

WHAT WALL PREPARATION IS NECESSARY?

A smooth, clean, dry, mildew-free wall does count. If your wall isn't in good condition, the prettiest paint color won't compensate. Before you even think about starting to paint, scrape or sand away rough spots. If necessary, strip old wallpaper. Depending on the paper and how it was applied, you may find a spray-on liquid combined with scoring to be less cumbersome than renting a steamer. If you do rent a steamer, follow the directions carefully to avoid accidents. If any glossy surfaces remain, dull them with sandpaper or liquid sandpaper. Scrub walls with mild detergent and water. Rinse with a sponge and clear water. For mold and mildew, wash with a solution of 1 quart household bleach and 3 quarts of water.

For the smoothest finish, always prime and treat spots with a special primer that prevents bleed-through. Don't ever paint over damp or wet walls. If the weather dampens the walls inside or out, run an air-conditioner or dehumidifier or wait for a dry day.

HOW DO THE PROS PAINT WALLS?

The best materials pay off in a professional-looking job. Purchase quality primers, paints, brushes, and rollers. A top-quality paint rolls on smoothly and evenly and has the depth of color lacking in some bargain paints. Latex paints are the norm today for most interior paint jobs. They are easy to apply, and brushes and rollers clean up with soap

and water. However, because it's tough and durable, consider oil-based paint for kitchen or bath cabinets.

If you are using a synthetic roller cover, precondition it by rinsing with water and spinning dry. (Do not precondition a lamb's-wool roller.) Use a metal tray, with disposable plastic liners, as it's more stable than a paint can and can be attached to a ladder. Fill only one-third of the tray with paint. Load the roller by rolling it in the deeper end of the tray, then smoothing it on the sloping surface until the paint is distributed evenly. Paint the ceiling first, starting with a narrow strip at the ceiling line, then walls around openings and along the baseboards. Use a brush, edging roller, or paint pad for this; use a small brush or trim roller for corners.

When applying paint to large surfaces, make a letter M (3 feet across and 3 feet high), then fill in spaces, working from the unpainted area into the wet paint. If you are using the same paint for walls and woodwork, paint the woodwork as you get to it. If the woodwork will be another color, paint it after you have completed the walls.

SPECIAL CASES: CHECKERBOARD FLOORS

Paint (two colors of oil-based enamel or floor paint)
Wood filler
Hand sander
Tack rags
Straightedge
Gray charcoal pencil
Chalk line
Quick-release masking tape (1 ¹⁄₂ inches wide)
Acrylic matte medium
Matte-finish, nonyellowing polyurethane
• **Measure** your room.
• **Transfer the measurements** to graph paper and chart out a check repeat that minimizes partial checks around the edges.
• **To prepare floor,** fill gaps with wood

filler and sand smooth. To make the job easier, rent a small hand sander for do-it-yourself projects. A commercial sander for floor refinishing is difficult to handle.

• *Pick up* sanding residue with a tack rag.
• *Paint the entire floor* in the lighter shade. Let dry.
• *Sand lightly.* Pick up sanding residue again with a tack rag.
• *Mark your pattern only* along the floor edges, using a straightedge and gray charcoal pencil.
• *Stretch a chalk line* across the room between the markings; snap lines to create the pattern.
• *Tape off darker squares* using 1 ½-inch-wide, quick-release masking tape.
• *Rub edges to secure* tape to the floor.
• *For a clean edge,* spread a light coat of acrylic matte medium available at art supply stores along the edge of the masking tape.
• *Paint the squares* with two coats of the darker color of your choice.
• *Allow adequate drying time* between coats. Seal with two coats of matte-finish, nonyellowing polyurethane.

SPECIAL CASES: STRIPED WALLS

*Painter's masking tape for
    decorative painting*
Carpenter's level
Measuring tape
Primer
Two shades latex wall paint
Pencil
Paint brushes

• *Decide how wide* you want stripes (probably from 2 to 4 inches).
• *Prime walls* with a premium-bond primer. After they dry, paint on a base coat. Allow to dry to avoid smudging.
• *Measure and mark stripes* on the wall with a pencil, using the level to ensure straight lines. Don't erase or you'll smudge the wall.
• *Mask off every other stripe* with tape, as follows. Carefully mask the outer edge of each pencil mark with quality painter's masking tape. Tightly seal down the edge next to the pencil lines with your fingers to prevent the paint from bleeding through. Test a small area first to be safe.
• *Paint the stripes of bare wall* exposed in between the masked-off stripes. Use smooth, even strokes.
• *After the color is applied,* gently remove the tape before the paint dries, being careful not to smear it.

SPECIAL CASES: SPONGING

Primer
Paint (two or more shades)
Natural sea sponges
Pie tin

• *Apply a primer or extra coat* of your base paint for a smooth finish.
• *Paint a solid base coat* and let dry overnight. Don't rush drying.
• *Test your technique* and color combination in a hidden place on a wall or on scrap board.
• *Wear disposable plastic gloves* instead of household rubber gloves, which leave fingerprint impressions. Change gloves as needed.
• *Use natural sea sponges* (not synthetic) to achieve a soft, mottled look. Vary the sizes for interesting effects.
• *Wet your sponge* with water, wringing it out thoroughly. This makes the paint adhere better to the sponge.
• *Pour a small amount of paint* into an old plate or pie tin and dip the sponge into it.
• *Cover the sponge* with a small amount of paint–too much will weigh it down. Use a newspaper to blot excess.
• *Cup the sponge* in your hand and push lightly onto the surface. Practice first.
• *Space the patches of color* evenly, but change the position of the sponge for an irregular, mottled effect. Close, overlapping marks have a sleek look; widely spaced sponging with little or no overlap produces a casual appearance. Try spacing first, then fill in as you prefer.
• *To apply several layers of color*, dab the first color over the base coat. Let it dry completely. Apply the second and third layers, drying in between.

SPECIAL CASES: PAINTING WOOD PANELING

Sandpaper and tack cloths
Liquid sandpaper
Shellac or clear lacquer
Alkyd primer
Latex paint

• *Sand paneling to remove* the gloss and wipe with tack cloths. Or apply liquid sandpaper, a deglossing agent.
• *Seal knots in paneling* with shellac or clear lacquer. Let dry completely.
• *Brush on an alkyd primer tinted* to match your paint color; allow to dry.
• *Apply one or two thin coats* of latex paint.

SPECIAL CASES: FAUX TILED WALL

Eggshell finish, off-white latex paint
Eggshell finish, white latex paint (quart)
Two shades of latex paint in your colors
Straightedge and level
Two small rollers
Small paint brushes

• *Start* with a light, clean wall; paint off-white if necessary.
• *If wall is freshly painted,* allow to dry thoroughly. Using a straightedge, level, white paint, and small brush, freehand paint the mortar lines that will divide 4×4-inch tiles. (See page 50.) Paint the mortar lines freehand–don't tape–to keep the effect loose and casual. For easy spacing, start at center of each wall and work out.
• *Using a smaller roller* for each color, paint inside the mortar lines. While the paint is still wet, brush over each "tile," using separate brushes for each color.
• *Allow the painted wall* to dry thoroughly. Thin leftover off-white paint with acrylic urethane and brush over the walls for a color-washed effect.

INDEX & CREDITS

Pages 8-11 *Design by:Randy Johnson and Steve Anderson, Birmingham, Alabama; photography: Cheryl Dalton, Atlanta, Georgia.*
Pages 12-13 *Paint (no. 3/C 300 and 4/F 202) courtesy of Benjamin Moore & Co. (800-826-2623); photography: Greg Scheideman/Studio AU, Des Moines, Iowa.*
Pages 14-17 *Photography: Greg Scheidman.*
Pages 22-27, 50-51 *Design by Urban Country, Bethesda, Maryland; photography: Gordon Beall, Washington, D.C.*
Pages 34-35 *Design by Sarah Boyer Jenkins, Chevy Chase, Maryland; photography: Gordon Beall.*
Pages 52-53 *Design by Gari Rogers, Birmingham, Alabama; photography: Cheryl Dalton.*
Page 59 *Design by JDS Designs Inc., Washington, D.C.; photography: Gordon Beall.*
Pages 72-73 *Design by Brown-Davis, Washington, D.C.; photography: Gordon Beall.*
Pages 104-107 *Design by Beverly Broun Alexandria, Virginia.*

U.S. UNITS TO METRIC EQUIVALENTS

To Convert From	Multiply By	To Get
Inches	25.4	Millimeters (mm)
Inches	2.54	Centimeters (cm)
Feet	30.48	Centimeters (cm)
Feet	0.3048	Meters (m)

METRIC UNITS TO U.S. EQUIVALENTS

To Convert	Multiply By	To Get
Millimeters	0.0394	Inches
Centimeters	0.3937	Inches
Centimeters	0.0328	Feet
Meters	3.2808	Feet